Church:
Why Bother?

A Study in 1 Timothy

A Woodside Bible Church Publication

Contributing authors:

Rob Bentz, Nathan Didlake,
Lauren Frith, Kevin Pobursky,
Dan Stewart, Tiffani Zale

TABLE OF CONTENTS

A Note from Pastor Chris Brooks
"Church. Why bother?"

It's a question many ask in our culture today. We often wonder, can I be spiritual without attending church? Or can I have a personal relationship with Jesus without the complexities of in-person religion? What about the problem of church abuse? With all this in mind, why should we bother with church?

Maybe you've asked some of these questions too.

Friends, God has a beautiful design for His church. A family—brothers and sisters, mothers and fathers—walking alongside each other as we hold on to gospel truth in the chaos of this world. My prayer is that through this resource, you will be impacted by the truth of Scripture that speaks to this beautiful, intricate design.

The book of 1 Timothy speaks to these truths. And if each of us submits to them, our church will function as the loving family God intends. One that beautifully represents the truth of God's merciful plan of salvation through Jesus. That is why we bother.

As you utilize this resource, I invite you to spend time each week reading a chapter of 1 Timothy and answering the questions in this book that correspond with that chapter of Scripture. Start your times of study with prayer, asking that the Holy Spirit of God will help you understand the spiritual truth you are reading (1 Corinthians 2:9-13).

Then, when you meet in your Life Group, discuss what you read using the "For Life Group Discussion" section.

We are excited to begin this journey as a church family, both individually and together in corporate worship. May God bless us and strengthen our faith and relationships for His glory in this world!

Soli Deo Gloria,

Pastor Chris Brooks
Senior Pastor – Woodside Bible Church

Context for the Book of 1 Timothy

Family drama is always hard to stomach. It can ruin holiday gatherings, add strain to life's milestones, and wear us down over time. Watching loved ones hurt each other with bad behavior is disheartening. One can rationalize it when people are younger and immature, but what should you do when people who should know better behave sinfully? And how do you correct the wrong thinking that justifies wrong behavior?

These were the sorts of questions Timothy faced while leading the Ephesian church. The church is a spiritual family; even here, family drama can happen.

Acts 15:36–18:23 tells us about Paul's second missionary journey, during which Timothy traveled as part of his team. Their group stayed for quite some time in the city of Ephesus, building the church there. Later, as Paul moved on to other cities, he left Timothy behind to lead the church in Ephesus and structure it in a sustainable way. 1 Timothy is a book originally written as a letter from the Apostle Paul to Timothy to encourage and instruct him. It was also intended to be read to the whole church.

In chapter 1, Paul tells Timothy to fight against false teachers seeking to bring bad theology (and thus, bad lifestyles) into the church. The rest of the book reveals how the church, the "household of God" (3:15), can function as a family that demonstrates the Gospel of Jesus Christ to the world.

Tips for Life Group Leaders

Church: Why Bother? A Study in 1 Timothy is a book intended for personal Bible study and small group discussion. Please encourage the members of your Life Group to obtain their own copy and complete the weekly lessons. Doing so will enable them to establish rhythms of time in God's Word each week.

This resource is written in such a way that the answers to the individual questions completed in each chapter become the first part of your discussion as a group. You will notice that the last part of each chapter is a section called "For Life Group Discussion." You can use this section as a script to lead your Life Group meeting and discuss each chapter.

The book of 1 Timothy contains several tricky passages. Godly, biblical scholars have debated the interpretation and application of these passages for hundreds of years, especially in recent times, as questions about church authority and gender roles, among other issues, have risen to the level of cultural discussions.   Please be sensitive to the variety of experiences and interpretations that might be present among people in your Life Group. Invite the group into honest discussions but, as often as possible, direct people to speak about what they see in Scripture rather than merely sharing their experiences or opinions.

Above all, establish the expectation that, even in disagreement of interpretation and opinion, the group will be united in love for one another through the love of Christ Jesus. Your own interactions with the group will create this culture, so ask the Holy Spirit to give you great wisdom (and be encouraged because God will give it to you generously! See James 1:5).

1 Timothy 1
The Church Upholds the Gospel

"I am writing these things to you so that...you may know how one ought to behave in the household of God, which is the church of the living God, a pillar and buttress of truth." -1 Timothy 3:14-15

"The aim of our charge is love that issues from a pure heart and a good conscience and a sincere faith." -1 Timothy 1:5

Imagine what it would be like to live in a home where the parents never told their children "No." Every child on the planet would sign up to live there! The children would be happy and content as long as they always got their own way. But would they be safe? Would they learn to work out solutions to their disagreements? Would they learn to seek the mutual good of the whole family?

Loving parents know they must suffer the short-term tears of an angry child who doesn't get her way to achieve the long-term goal of a peaceful household for all.

Do parents tell a child "No" because they don't love or respect her? Quite the opposite—they love her so much that they are invested in ensuring she grows up to be the best human being possible. They want her to thrive in the world. To this end, they deliver both encouragement and correction along the way. And as parents help each of their children grow into maturity, they ensure that the entire household benefits from these actions of love for one another.

In 1 Timothy, Paul says that the church is the "household" of God (3:15). We are family! There are ways that we can behave in this household that will ensure the good of all.

Our church family is related through Jesus Christ and the salvation He achieved for us through His life, death, and resurrection. The truth of who God is and how He saves is something we will recount to each other for all of eternity. It is what sets the church apart in the world, and it is the message of hope that we offer the world. The way that we treat each other holds high on display the truth of God's glorious gospel.

Read 1 Timothy 1
⇨ Observe

1. This book is a personal letter from Paul to Timothy. What does Paul call Timothy in 1:2 (and again in 1:18) that gives us insight into the nature of their relationship?

2. Turn to 1 Timothy 3 and read verses 14-16. Record the purpose of this letter: Paul wrote to Timothy, "so that" what? And what "mystery" is he revealing?

3. Paul is charging Timothy to correct people who are teaching a false gospel in the church. What does 1:5 say is the aim of this charge?

4. In chapter 1, Paul explains that Timothy's conduct and teaching must align with the gospel to enforce his stand against false teachers. List the words Paul uses in 1:5, 11, 12, and 19 AND in 3:14-16 to drive home this point (hint: look for synonyms for "conduct" and "teaching").

5. Read 1:15-16. Describe how Paul sees himself and how he views what Jesus has done for him.

6. Look up Romans 2:4. How does this verse help you understand the patience of God and its effect in your life?

✋ Understand and Apply

7. Paul says that the church is the "household" of God (3:15), holding up the truth of God. How does Paul and Timothy's relationship show us how we should relate to those in God's household?
See also Philippians 2:19-22.

8. What can you do this week to lean into your spiritual family at church, to either care for someone else's needs or rely on someone to meet yours?

9. In 3:16, the word "mystery" could better be interpreted as "secret," something that was once concealed that is now revealed. The world thinks that the secret to godliness, or being aligned with God, depends on the morals or rituals we do to move toward God. Paul's explanation is very different. Reread 1:15 and 3:16. Who is doing the moving in these verses? And who is He moving toward?

So what is the "secret" of being aligned with God?

10. God came to us in Jesus! Jesus moved toward sinners, and when He saves us, He moves our hearts to do the same. Who is it in your life that needs you to move toward them with the secret of the gospel?

Find hope in the patience of Jesus (1:16)—there is still time for anyone living to believe in him for eternal life!

11. Why is it loving to correct someone's false teaching about the true Gospel? Reread 1:6-7 and 1:19-20 for more insight.

12. How do you ensure that YOU are living and believing "in accordance with the glorious gospel of the blessed God" (1:11) and upholding truth (3:15)? What action steps can we derive from Paul's instructions to Timothy in chapter 1?

✟ Theology Spotlight
HOW DO THE LAW AND THE GOSPEL FIT TOGETHER?

Christians can often be confused about our relationship to the Old Testament Law. Are we responsible for following the Law after Jesus came to live and die for us and make us right with God? Paul doesn't see the Law and the Gospel in contrast with each other. In 1 Timothy 1:8-11, he tells us that "the law is good, if one uses it lawfully—in accordance with the glorious gospel of the blessed God."

Ezekiel 36:26-28 gives us insight into this. God said, "I will give you a new heart, and a new spirit I will put within you, and cause you to walk in my statutes and be careful to obey my rules, and you shall be my people, and I will be your God."

Jesus didn't bring us a new law so much as He gives us new hearts when we trust Him to forgive our sins. The new hearts He gives us are able to receive, understand, and obey the heart of the law through the power of the Holy Spirit in us!

Summary

The church is the family of God. We hold up the truth of the gospel as God's people. What a joy and a privilege! To be faithful to this task, it is essential to define what is and is not the true gospel. In doing so, we demonstrate love for our spiritual family. We will love each other too much to let anyone "swerve" off course or "shipwreck" their faith. We will offer the world the true gospel, in contrast to "speculations" and "vain discussions," because we live with sincere faith holding tight to the message of Jesus's salvation of sinners.

Prayer

Use this page to process the Lord's work in your heart through written prayer. Respond to the following prompts or write your own prayer of response.

- Copy the text of 1 Timothy 1:15 below.
- Then reflect on it and pray it aloud.
- What changes your perception of yourself when you say these words?
- What changes about your perception of Jesus, considering verse 16 as well?
- Paul breaks out in praise to God after pondering his salvation (verse 17). Write your own prayer of praise for who God is and what He has done.

Use the following questions to guide your discussion of chapter 1 in your Life Group meeting.

Icebreaker

Share a time when someone corrected you or stopped you from doing something because they loved you. What trouble or danger did they save you from?

Chapter Review

Paul is writing to Timothy, his son in the faith. He is writing with instructions about how to conduct himself and lead the church to behave so that the gospel of God will be clearly shown to the world. In this case, it meant that Timothy was going to have to correct some people in the church about the way they were teaching the Gospel. Paul reminds him of the true Gospel and that if we live with sincere faith and a good conscience, we will demonstrate the truth through our love for others.

Have someone read 1 Timothy 1 aloud to the group from the ESV.

Discussion Questions

1. What stood out to you from your answers to questions #7-12 in the "Understand and Apply" section?

2. What does Paul mean in 1:20 that he has "handed over to Satan" those who "have made shipwreck of their faith" (1:19)?

No clear answer is given in Scripture, but we can gain insight from Matthew 18:17, where Jesus tells us what to do with a brother or sister who won't receive correction from the church. **Read Matthew 18:17.** What should the person who won't receive correction become to us instead of like family?

Now turn to Matthew 9:11-12. How did Jesus treat tax collectors and sinners?

How, then, should our behavior and intentions change toward those who prove not to be members of the family of God because they teach a false gospel?

What questions do you still have about 1 Timothy 1? How will you seek answers?

Take a few minutes of solitude for everyone to answer these questions individually before sharing them as a group.

What is God saying to you through your study of 1 Timothy 1?

How will you step out in obedience through the power of the Holy Spirit?

Prayer

"King of ages, immortal, invisible, the only God, be honor and glory [to you] forever" (1:17). We praise you for our salvation, Lord! We are so grateful for your patient mercy in our lives and that you have saved us through Jesus. Please help us live with our spiritual family, the church, in love and truth. Give us spiritual discernment to recognize when we may be swerving from your true Gospel, and give us the courage to, when necessary, lovingly guide a brother or sister toward truth. We know that we are sinners saved by grace, so help us to accept correction humbly from the members of our spiritual household. May the truth of your gospel be lifted high through our church!

1 Timothy 2
A Holy, Praying Church

"First of all, then, I urge that supplications, prayers, intercessions, and thanksgivings be made for all people..." -1 Timothy 2:1

"I desire then that in every place the men should pray, lifting holy hands without anger or quarreling..." -1 Timothy 2:8

People from the south are known for their distinctive drawl. It's the mark of a proper southerner to say things like y'all, and I reckon. And if you grew up in the south, you're probably used to hearing speech thick as molasses and long as the Texas plains. Imagine you're in church on a Sunday morning, and a proper Texan walks through the doors, fully dressed in a Stetson, a large golden belt buckle, pleated denim, and a starched bright white dress shirt. He casually throws a "Howdy" towards another 500-gallon hat-doating friend on the way in, but when called upon to pray, he stands before the church and suddenly speaks in perfect Old King James. The man looks like he'd ridden into church on a prize-winning horse after a morning of boot-scooting. But now, he's morphed into thees and thous. He sounds like he's reciting a Shakespearean sonnet! What's happening?

There are many aspects to being a church community, the preaching of God's word, prayer, small groups, worship, missions, and events, amongst many other things. Each can be done in a way that pleases or displeases God. In the same way that we might find it preposterous to hear a southern cowboy speak like a Shakespearean poet, God finds it preposterous when His church prays without holy hands.

In his desire to help Timothy structure the Ephesian church, Paul begins with a matter of deepest importance—holy prayer should be done by people whose hearts are holy. 1 Timothy 2 addresses the idea that people can do God's work in an ungodly way. Our acts of Christian devotion should pour out of the holiness God gives us. However, this isn't always the reality within the church. Before a church can hope to have a good structure (as we will see in 1 Timothy 3), they must first learn to do the foundational work of the church—prayer. Paul's call for righteous prayer is for us too.

Read 1 Timothy 2
⇨ Observe

1. 1 Timothy 2:1 begins with the primary tasks of the church. What are those tasks?

2. What are the differences between "supplications, prayers, intercessions, and thanksgivings?" Are these four different things or four aspects of the same thing, like four corners of the same square? (It may help to look up the words in a dictionary or Bible glossary).

3. Who does Paul call the church to pray for (2:1-2), and how does Paul's role as a teacher of the Gentiles (2:7) add an emphasis to his call?

4. What does 1 Timothy 2:3-7 reveal about God's heart for all people?

5. Revisit 1 Timothy 2:5-6. How is Jesus described in these verses? What do you think is the significance of Jesus being described as a "mediator" and a "ransom for all?"

6. In 1 Timothy 2:8–15, Paul reiterates the church's call to corporate prayer for all people (2:1). How does Paul instruct the men to pray (2:8)? How should the women pray (2:9–10)?

✋ Understand and Apply

7. Paul begins his instructions to the Ephesian church on how to pray well. What does this instruction tell us about the primary importance of prayer in the church's life?

8. Consider who is included in all peoples (2:1). How should people who disagree with current political leaders (or even local church leaders) approach God on their behalf in prayer? Are there any other people groups you struggle to bring to God in prayer? Why or why not?

9. Paul uses a significant metaphor in his call for prayer in 1 Timothy 2:8–10. What are the physical differences between fighting hands and praying hands? What are the physical differences between gaudy adornments to show off and the adornment of good, righteous works?

10. What heart issues lie behind the men's inability to pray (in 2:8) and the women's inability to pray (in 2:9–10)?

11. How does Paul's corrective instruction for men and women apply to you right now?

12. In chapter 3, Paul will begin to talk about the structure of church leadership. If a church has a good structure but does not have a culture of prayer, what do you think the Apostle Paul would have to say to that church?

✝ Theology Spotlight
WHAT IS PAUL TEACHING ABOUT WOMEN IN THE CHURCH?

Paul is writing this letter to Timothy, who leads a real church with real people facing real problems. So, to better understand 1 Timothy 2:8-15, we need to separate the principles Paul is commending to all churches for corporate worship from the specific examples he addresses in the church of Ephesus where Timothy was leading.

Paul is instructing the church to pray (2:1) and gives examples of the heart attitudes with which all people are to be in prayer: with holiness, gentleness (2:8), and with humility and self-control (2:9). All people, as seen in the men in the Ephesian church, will be tempted to quarrel (2:8), and all people, as seen in the women in the Ephesian church, will be tempted to use their appearance to gain approval from others (2:9-10). But as members of God's family, we want to live differently. By focusing on living "peaceful and quiet lives" of prayer, "godly and dignified in every way" (2:2), we can avoid becoming, or listening to, false teachers (1:18-19) that swerve away from the truth.

Paul's directive to "let a woman learn" (2:11) was countercultural in its day. Women in most other religious systems were not invited to learn. However, Paul is connecting the importance of learning with the ability to profess and live out godliness in the Christian faith(2:10). The qualifying statement "in quietness with all submissiveness" (2:11) is consistent with the lives that Paul is calling all believers to live (2:2), not clamoring for the authority to teach without proper understanding—which leads to false teaching (1:7).

In 1 Timothy 2:12-15, Paul appeals to God's purposes and promises in the creation account in Genesis to remind the Ephesian church that submission to God in corporate worship is good and necessary (2:3). Faithful Christians differ in their interpretation of 1 Timothy 2:12. Some claim that "a man" refers to all men in general. Others believe that Paul is referring back to "the man Christ Jesus" from 2:5. Some understand the passage to prohibit women from teaching in a way that undermines the appointed godly leadership of the church. In any case, Paul's call to women is to maintain a posture of submission to the authority of Christ and the true Gospel (2:4, 1:3).

1 Timothy 2:5 shows Paul clearly stating salvation is through Christ Jesus alone. So the phrase "she will be saved through childbearing" (2:15) may refer to the promise of God in Genesis 3:14-15 that Eve would bear a child who would crush

the serpent's head. Through the birth, life, death, and resurrection of Jesus, all people are saved and can "continue in faith and love and holiness, with self-control" (2:15).

Summary

Before a church can really think about its leadership and structure, it must learn to pray. God's heart is that all people come to the saving knowledge of His Son. God has called His church to share His heart with all people. As a church is called to pray, it must enter prayer with hearts that reflect the holiness of God. Men and women, called into a holy calling, are called into this holy task since God loves all people—and desires that all be saved.

Prayer

Use this page to process the Lord's work in your heart through written prayer. Respond to the following prompts or write your own prayer of response.

- Begin by asking God to guide your prayer. Ask that He would change any heart postures that detract from the holy act of prayer.
- Copy the text of 1 Timothy 2:1-2 below.
- Reflect upon who it is in your life needs supplication prayer. Who needs intercession? For whom can you give thanks? What rulers and leaders in your life (liked or disliked) need prayer?
- Make a list of these people and slowly bring their needs before the Lord.
- Finally, write a prayer of intercession for the hearts of the people within your church. Pray for hearts that live out the holiness God has given to them. Pray for prayerful hearts that reflect God's loving-kindness.

Use the following questions to guide your discussion of chapter 2 in your Life Group meeting.

Icebreaker

Have you ever heard someone speak one way in normal conversation and then a completely different way when they were praying? What were the differences? And how did that impact your ability to pray alongside this person?

Chapter Review

Paul is writing to Timothy, his protégé commissioned to bring theological and structural order to the Ephesian church. In 1 Timothy 2, Paul starts with a matter of first importance: that the Ephesian church should pray—and that their prayer should reflect the holiness God has given to them. Paul calls for prayer for all people (including leadership) by all of God's people, men and women. Based on this call to prayer, Paul begins to address specific issues the Ephesian men and women were facing that were standing in the way of effective prayer.

Have someone read 1 Timothy 2 aloud for the group out of the ESV version.

Discussion Questions

1. What stood out to you from your answers to questions #7-12 in the "Understand and Apply" section?

2. In 1 Timothy 2:1, Paul instructs the church to make *supplications, prayers, intercessions, and thanksgiving* for *all people*. What does this mean? Have you participated in doing this? Alone or with the church?

Read Matthew 6:5-8. In this passage, Jesus is teaching His followers how to pray. How is His instruction similar to that of Paul's? How should both teachings impact our prayer life personally and as the church?

Read Matthew 6:9-13. How do you see Paul's instructions for prayer (supplication, intercession, and thanksgiving) reflected in the prayer Jesus modeled for us? How does this further illuminate what you've learned in 1 Timothy?

3. What questions do you still have about 1 Timothy 2? How will you seek answers?

4. Take a few minutes of solitude for everyone to answer these questions individually before sharing them as a group.

What is God saying to you through your study of 1 Timothy 2?

How will you step out in obedience through the power of the Holy Spirit?

Prayer

Dear God, our Savior, who gave your Son Jesus as a ransom for all, please focus our hearts on prayer now and throughout each day. We need you to change our hearts from quarrelsome and selfish to quiet and humble. We pray for those in authority over us, even those we may disagree with. You know their needs, and we pray that you will meet them. We know that you desire all people to be saved, so we ask you to save our leaders through Jesus. And, Lord, please let our church be a place of prayer and holiness that reflects your loving heart.

1 Timothy 3
Qualified leaders watch over and care for the church

"The saying is trustworthy: If anyone aspires to the office of overseer, he desires a noble task." -1 Timothy 3:1

"For those who serve well as deacons gain a good standing for themselves and also great confidence in the faith that is in Christ Jesus." -1 Timothy 3:13

Have you ever desired to do something significant like run for public office, join the school board, or become the president of your HOA? Or maybe you've longed to start your own business because you recognize you have expertise in an area that can make a difference for others or an idea that can lead to a product that will help people in a new, beneficial way.

Whatever the truly important thing you desire to do, what would you consider to be the first step in making it a reality? Would you focus on the tasks to be done? For example, if running for public office, would you think first of the money you need to raise, the people you need to employ on your campaign, or the office space you'd need to secure?

Or would you focus on the person you need to be to perform this service? Would you consider why you want to serve the public, your values, and your responsibilities? Would you ask yourself the hard question of whether or not you have the strong character needed for such a role?

In 1 Timothy 3, Paul writes to Timothy to give him a character profile for those who provide leadership in the church: elders and deacons. Paul doesn't provide Timothy with task-driven job descriptions for these roles but instead outlines the kind of people they should be. According to Paul, church leaders should have lives shaped by the Gospel, as the Holy Spirit consistently works through character before talent. A humble heart of service, a patient spirit, a kind heart. Things like service must lie at the heart of Christian leadership because the Church's foremost leader, Jesus Christ, led from the heart of a servant.

Read 1 Timothy 3
⇨ Observe

1. In 1 Timothy, Paul says, "The saying is trustworthy..." (1:15, 3:1, 4:9). In 1:15 and 4:9, Paul draws attention to the assurance of salvation we have in Jesus. What insight does this give us into the weight of the character traits Paul outlines for elders and deacons? (Note: The terms "overseer" and "elder" are used interchangeably in Scripture.)

2. List the character traits of elders (3:1-7). Do you observe any pattern? Can they be grouped? If so, how?

3. List the character traits of deacons (3:8-10 and 12-13). Do you observe any pattern? Can these be grouped? If so, how?

4. Look at the character traits of an overseer and a deacon again. What similarities and differences do you see?

5. Read 1 Peter 5:1-4. How does what Peter says about elders deepen your understanding of the role of an elder in the church?

6. Read Acts 6:1-7 which describes the first deacons in the New Testament. What were the seven men appointed to do? What did their appointment free up the apostles for? What was the result (hint: see v. 7)?

✋ Understand and Apply

7. Paul describes "who" an elder is by identifying the character that they should have. How would you describe what an elder does? See also 1 Peter 5:1-5.

8. The terms elder, overseer, and pastor are used interchangeably in the New Testament (see Acts 20:17, 28; Titus 1:5-7; 1 Peter 1-5). How does this feature give further insight into the function of an elder?

9. The New Testament gives us a model of elders existing as a plurality, i.e., more than one (see Acts 16:4, 20:17; Titus 1:5; James 5:14). What are the benefits of a shared leadership structure in the church? How does a shared leadership structure promote stronger accountability and healthier responsibility?

10. How do the roles of the elder and deacon work together to lead the church? (Refer back to Acts 6:1-7.)

11. Paul lists characteristics of those who will lead in the local church, but it is essentially a list of traits that should be present in every Christian's life. To what extent are they descriptive of you? In what areas of your life are you encouraged? In what areas do you need change?

✝ Theology Spotlight

IS PAUL LEAVING WOMEN OUT?

Paul is writing this letter to Timothy, who leads a real church with real people facing real problems. So, to better understand 1 Timothy 2:8-15, we need to separate the principles Paul is commending to all churches for corporate worship from the specific examples he addresses in the church of Ephesus where Timothy was leading.

In 1 Timothy 3, Paul speaks about church leadership roles. He states that the role of elder, which is a teaching and governing (oversight) role, is specifically assigned to faithful men who are above reproach (1 Tim. 3:1-7; Titus 1:5-9). Whether the role of deacon is open to women as well as men has been debated (see suggested reading on page ___), depending on the interpretation and implications of verses 8-13.

With this distinction along gender lines, there is danger in embracing a divisive heart posture in the church that is inconsistent with the heart of Christ. Paul's reminder that the church is the "household" of God (3:15) concludes his remarks on the offices of elders and deacons, reminding us that we are family. As sisters and brothers in God's household, women and men are equal in worth, joint heirs of salvation through faith in Christ, and endowed by the Holy Spirit with spiritual gifts to serve the body of believers and to reach the world with the Gospel.

The value of women is not diminished because the Bible reserves the role of elder for men. Throughout Scripture, it is clear that women are loved by God, worthy of honor, and play key roles in God's kingdom plans. We can see from Romans 16:1-18 and Philippians 4:3 that Paul, specifically, values women as fellow workers for the gospel, worthy saints, and dear sisters.

When it comes to leadership in the church, we must be aware of the tremendous influence that our own life experience, history of denominational practice and tradition, and personal preferences have had on our practice and beliefs. Psalm 25:5 is a great prayer for our hearts as we study difficult topics like this: "Lead me by your truth and teach me, for you are the God who saves me. All day long I put my hope in you" (NIV).

Paul is not leaving women out. Men and women equally display the image of God, and both are important for the ministry of the church to flourish and for the glory of God to be reflected in a broken world.

Summary

The church is the family of God, and it is led by qualified leaders who demonstrate the character of Christ in heart and deed. Often we focus too narrowly on what leaders do rather than on who they are. Any church that selects leaders based on their talents or abilities alone will come to ruin. Instead, churches should appoint leaders that have characters shaped by the gospel. The gospel is the motivating factor for Paul's character profile for elders and deacons in 1 Timothy 3—a character that prioritizes service over status and love over power. Gifts and abilities can be considered, but they are both less important than character. When the character of church leaders is aligned with the gospel, its transforming power is displayed.

Prayer

Use this page to process the Lord's work in your heart through written prayer. Respond to the following prompts or write your own prayer of response.

- Copy the text of 1 Timothy 3:9-10 below.
- Reflect on the spiritual requirements for leaders in the church and how their lifestyle must align with their understanding of the gospel.
- Ask God to provide godly, tested leaders to serve our church.
- Write a prayer asking God to work out v. 9-10 in your life—that you would continue to gain spiritual understanding. Take the time to confess your sin that does not allow you to live with a clear conscience.
- Thank God for the grace that overflows for you in Christ Jesus (1:14).

Use the following questions to guide your discussion of chapter 3 in your Life Group meeting.

Icebreaker

Think of an example of a job or role in an organization (e.g., teacher, salesman, tradesman, manager, etc.). It could be the job you have currently or another. Describe the ideal candidate. Then discuss: What is the focus of your description?

Chapter Review

Timothy is a young leader in the church in Ephesus. There are issues arising in the church stemming from false teachers that promoted speculation rather than faithful stewardship of the gospel. The resulting effect on the believers was less than edifying. Paul, Timothy's mentor, writes to encourage his young pastor in fulfilling his calling as an officer of the church. To that end, Paul describes to Timothy the character traits that elders (overseers) and deacons should have so that the church will stay true to the gospel and faithfully steward the doctrine given to them.

Have someone read 1 Timothy 3 aloud to the group from the ESV.

Discussion Questions

1. What stood out to you from your answers to questions #7-11 in the "Understand & Apply" section?

2. In 1 Timothy 3:2, Paul says that overseers must be "above reproach," and verse 10 says that deacons must "prove themselves blameless." Is Paul calling leaders to be perfect? Probably not! So what can we expect to see in our leaders?

When Paul says in 5:22, "Do not be hasty in the laying on of hands, " he warns Timothy not to appoint someone to church leadership before they are ready. **Read 3:10.** What does this verse say about when someone is ready for leadership? What does this look like in life?

Turn to John 15:1-11 and have someone read it aloud. What will be seen in the life of a follower of Jesus (v. 2, 5)?

What fruit will God produce in us when we abide in him (see v. 9, 10, and 11)?

Consider the gardening process and how much time it takes to grow fruit. How does God use the circumstances of our lives to prune us and produce the character of Christ in us?

Scan 1 Timothy 3:1-13 again. The qualifications listed here can also be described as the "fruit" of following Jesus over time. How does this encourage you?

3. What questions do you still have about 1 Timothy 3? How will you seek answers?

4. Take a few minutes of solitude for everyone to answer these questions individually before sharing them as a group.

What is God saying to you through your study of 1 Timothy 3?

How will you step out in obedience through the power of the Holy Spirit?

Prayer

Father in heaven, you are lovely and holy in every way. In your infinite wisdom, you have called us into being. You have saved us through your Son by your matchless love and called us into the light of your glory. By the power of your Holy Spirit, may the character of our lives be shaped by the gospel. Grant us strength and courage to surrender to your work in our lives. May you raise up leaders among us who are patterned after your Son to be faithful stewards of your will by faith. And may we faithfully pray for the leaders you place in our lives for our good and your glory. Amen.

1 Timothy 4
Hold Tight to the Truth

"Have nothing to do with irreverent, silly myths. Rather train yourself for godliness; for while bodily training is of some value, godliness is of value in every way, as it holds promise for the present life and also for the life to come." -1 Timothy 4:7-8

If you've ever had a job where you regularly handled cash, you probably received some form of counterfeit bill training. This training teaches you how to identify fake money by first teaching you how to recognize the real thing. The National Mint has woven many unique details into its bills, making for authentic and true currency. If one of these details is missing, wrong, or added, we know it's a counterfeit. A fairly observant individual may be able to turn down an "Ome Hondred" dollar bill, but it takes some stronger training to be able to spot a more convincing phony. You may have seen a cashier hold a crisp hundred-dollar bill up to the light to look for the security thread inside that verifies its validity. Without that strip, it's just a piece of paper. Worthless.

In the same way, we as Christians need to be able to recognize and know the truth of God's Word. Being familiar with the scriptures helps us identify false teachings and ensures we don't exchange the most valuable thing we have, our faith, for something worthless!

In 1 Timothy 4, Paul warns Timothy against the false teachings happening in Ephesus, as some have departed from the truth. Paul's diligent training in the Word has equipped him to recognize the misleading things being taught as holy practices immediately. He instructs Timothy to remember the training he's given and continue training, pursuing godliness. This is the only training that has lasting value, "for while bodily training is of some value, godliness is of value in every way, as it holds promise for the present life and also for the life to come" (1 Timothy 4:8).

Paul's instructions to Timothy are for us too! As believers, we must continue to affirm the truth of God's Word, train in righteousness, and devote ourselves to the Scriptures, so that we might stay on course and not depart from the faith! By doing so, we also set an example for other believers and are able to bring correction to false teachings by way of the truth.

Read 1 Timothy 4

⇾ Observe

1. In 1 Timothy 4:1-5 Paul warns Timothy of those who have departed from the faith and have started to teach false things. What false teachings were mentioned, and what does Paul say in response to these practices?

2. Turn to Genesis 1 and skim the chapter. What phrase do you see repeated (v. 12, 18, 21, 25, 31)?

3. Read Ecclesiastes 9:7-9. How does this passage support Paul's argument against the false teaching in 1 Timothy 4:3-5?

4. In 1 Timothy 4:6 & 11, Paul uses the phrase "these things." What is he referring to?

5. Paul reminds Timothy that he has "trained" (4:6) but that he must still "train" (4:7) as he continues in his ministry. What is the training he is referring to, and what does he say the benefits of the training will be?

6. Reread 1 Timothy 4:12-16. Paul paints a picture here for Timothy of what training in godliness looks like. List some of the things he states.

✋ Understand and Apply

7. Paul recognized the false teaching that was happening in the church of Ephesus and sent Timothy to correct things. How was Paul able to recognize the lies being taught, and how did he refute them?

What does this teach you about the importance of knowing the scriptures?

8. In 1 Timothy 4:6, Paul tells Timothy he has been "trained in the word of faith and of the good doctrine." How does Timothy's previous training prepare him to help the church in Ephesus, and why do you think Paul encourages Timothy to continue training?

9. Read Psalm 119:9-16. How does this passage and your answer to the previous question impact your view of training in the faith?

What does *training in godliness* currently look like in your life, and what is the importance of continued training to you?

10. Write your best definition of godliness. (Feel free to look up the word in a dictionary or Bible glossary)

11. Revisit 1 Timothy 4:10 & 1 Timothy 3:16. Both refer to the gospel of Christ. How does the gospel give us a clearer picture and stronger purpose in our pursuit of godliness?

12. Paul instructs Timothy to live out his faith as an example to the church (4:12, 14-15) and to lead the church to do the same through publicly reading the Scriptures, encouraging and teaching them (4:13). How do you think these practices helped the church in Ephesus and the present church today?

_____

✟ Theology Spotlight
HOW ARE WE SAVED?

In Paul's original letter to the Ephesians, he explicitly tells them that salvation is a "free gift" from God and "not a result of works" (Ephesians 2:8-9). So, why does he tell Timothy in this letter that he must "toil and strive" towards godliness (1 Timothy 4:10)? And that by persisting in living out the faith, he will be able to "save" himself and his hearers? While this may sound confusing, Paul is not using the word "save" here to mean salvation but rather referring to being saved from false teachers. Paul encourages both Timothy and the early church to be diligent in the practicing of their faith so that they might not go astray or be deceived. Remember the opening line of this chapter: "The Spirit expressly says that in later times some will depart from the faith" (1 Timothy 4:1). Paul's command to train in godliness is something we can take to heart today as instruction for how to not depart from the faith.

_____

Summary

By holding tight to the Word of God and training in godliness, we can stand firm in our faith's truths and help others do the same. Paul is explicit in saying, "some will depart from the faith." Deception and false teaching are all around us. It takes dedication to the truth and continued practice of godliness to keep us on course.

Prayer

Use this page to process the Lord's work in your heart through written prayer. Respond to the following prompts or write your own prayer of response.

- Copy the text of 1 Timothy 4:10 below.
- Reflect upon what it means to *have your hope set on the living God.*
- How does this impact your drive to practice your faith?
- When do you struggle in your motivation to "practice," and how do those times impact your hope?
- Write a prayer of thanksgiving for our hope in God and of petition, asking God to help you remain motivated and vigilant as you practice godliness.

Use the following questions to guide your discussion of chapter 4 in your Life Group meeting.

Icebreaker

We've all heard the phrase "practice makes perfect." Share an example of something you've spent time practicing and how falling out of practice impacted that skill.

Chapter Review

Paul warns Timothy about those who have departed from the faith and are trying to enforce a false teaching. Paul sent Timothy to set the church of Ephesus straight by affirming the truth of the Gospel. He encourages Timothy to remember his training in the Word and urges him to continue training in godliness. By doing so, Timothy will be able to stand firm in the faith and be an example to the church that they, too, may continue in the way of the true gospel.

Have someone read 1 Timothy 4 aloud to the group from the ESV.

Discussion Questions

1. What stood out to you from your answers to questions #7-12 in the "Understand and Apply" section?

2. Paul tells Timothy to live a godly life and *set the believers an example in speech, conduct, love, faith, and purity* (1 Timothy 4:12). What do you think this means and looks like?

In many of Paul's letters to the early church, he shares similar instructions for living a life that bears evidence of a true faith. **Read Galatians 5:19-25**. How does this passage help paint a fuller picture of the example Paul called Timothy to set for the believers?

Now turn to 2 Peter 1:3-11. How is this passage similar to Paul's instruction to Timothy, and how does it expand upon what you've learned so far?

3. What questions do you still have about 1 Timothy 4? How will you seek answers?

4. Take a few minutes of solitude for everyone to answer these questions individually before sharing them as a group.

What is God saying to you through your study of 1 Timothy 4?

How will you step out in obedience through the power of the Holy Spirit?

Prayer

Living God, you are good, and we can set our hope on you! You have given us everything we need through the power of your Son and the truth of your Word to live a life of godliness. Thank you for your Word. Help us to hold tightly to it, to make the time to read it, and to know it by heart, so that we may stand firm in our faith. Please help us to be diligent in training in our faith. Make us more like you so that we might be an example to those around us, who may also see and know your truth. Amen

1 Timothy 5
The Family in the Church

"But if anyone does not provide for his relatives, and especially for members of his household, he has denied the faith and is worse than an unbeliever."
-1 Timothy 5:8

"Let the elders who rule well be considered worthy of double honor, especially those who labor in preaching and teaching." -1 Timothy 5:17

Family living can be complicated! When different genders, multiple generations, and unique backgrounds come under one roof, miscommunication and misunderstanding will abound! Introverts need personal space, while extroverts crave shared experiences. The kids communicate on virtual platforms, while the parents want to discuss things face-to-face. There are wars over the thermostat, fights over the remote control, and arguments over how long just one minute really takes. And the more people added to the household, the higher the tensions tend to get.

As we have already seen in 1 Timothy, the church is a family of faith, and as the family grows, so does the complexity. In chapter 5, Paul insists that members of the faith family should value and honor one another like a healthy family honors one another. An ungodly culture will tend to marginalize or devalue certain people, but the church is to be a place that expresses honor regardless of gender, age, or condition. Paul provides Timothy, and by extension, our church today, with a simple and clear concept of how to honor the various ages in the church.

Every family has unique complexities, which is also true in the church. The instructions and principles in this chapter provide guidance for displaying the transforming love of Jesus among the family of faith to the world.

Read 1 Timothy 5

⇨ Observe

1. Timothy is instructed to treat the members of the church as family members. What might it look like to treat each group mentioned here as family (older men as fathers, older women as mothers, younger men as brothers, younger women as sisters)?

How would this perspective promote purity in the church (5:2)?

2. Women in Paul's day had fewer options for work to support themselves, so when she lost her husband, she also lost her income. Who does Paul mention as responsible for caring for the various types of widows (5:3-4, 14)?

3. What expectation does Paul have for the older widows (5:5)? Younger widows (5:14)?

4. Paul has strong words for the family members who do not care for the vulnerable (such as widows) in their family (5:8). Who is responsible for providing for widows who have children or grandchildren?

5. How should the "elders who rule well" receive the honor they are due, according to verses 17-19?

6. Paul gave Timothy several warnings that would protect the church from harm that may come from church leaders who are not faithfully following Jesus. What guidelines does he give (5:20-21)?

✋ Understand and Apply

7. What practical ways can we provide for widows' needs in the church today?

8. When have you witnessed a widow devoting herself to good work (5:10)? How can an older widow serve in the church?

9. The description of the early church in Acts 6:1-7 suggests that their care for widows influenced the rapid growth of the church. Why might this have been, and could this be true today?

10. Think of the elders who lead and teach at your church. What could you do this week to show them the honor that this passage instructs?

11. Why did Paul give the somber charge about honoring elders "In the presence of God and of Christ Jesus and of the elect angels" (5:21)?

12. Re-read Paul's purpose statement for this letter to Timothy in chapter 3:14-16. How do these instructions for honoring our faith family in chapter 5 help us to function as "the church of the living God, a pillar and buttress of truth?"

✝ Theology Spotlight
IS THERE A DIFFERENCE BETWEEN "OLDER MEN" AND "ELDERS"?

The term translated "elders" in 1 Timothy 5:17 is the plural of the same word translated "older man" in 5:1. The context indicates, however, that verse 1 is referring to an "older man" who is mature in years, while verse 17 and following is referring to church leaders who were appointed to office according to the qualifications laid out in chapter three.

A man should not automatically be appointed to church leadership just because he is older in years. But the context of this chapter invokes the idea that every church elder should lead from the heart of a gracious father as he engages in the hard work of directing church affairs, preaching, and teaching. The exhortations in these verses to Timothy, the elders, and the church reveal the heavy responsibility that this role of elder/overseer carries.

Summary

Healthy relationships within the family of God are a priority. From the vulnerable to the leaders, family members are to be valued and honored through our care and treatment of each other. By embracing our collective responsibility for one another, the church experiences Christ's love and provision that He designed to sustain our witness to the truth and preserve our holiness as His body. We each have a role in fulfilling these responsibilities without partiality.

Prayer

Use this page to process the Lord's work in your heart through written prayer. Respond to the following prompts or write your own prayer of response.

- Copy the text of 1 Timothy 5:21 below.
- Then reflect on it and your faithfulness in living it.
- Ask God to fill you with a spirit of honoring all the family members in your church.
- God and the angels witness our treatment of our personal and faith family. Write a prayer for those in your family whom God brings to mind.

Use the following questions to guide your discussion of chapter 5 in your Life Group meeting.

Icebreaker

Share with the group one of the adjustments you learned to make as your family has grown or changed. What is different now since that change (for example, now that you are married, have children, have aging parents, live in a different community, etc.)?

Chapter Review

In chapter 5, Paul instructs Timothy on navigating relationships with people in the church of various ages and situations. After a general charge to treat one another with the honor one would in a healthy family, he specifically addresses the importance of honoring widows and church leaders. "Honor widows" is this chapter's longest and possibly most complex instruction. Paul describes a variety of situations and relevant guidelines for caring for them. "Honor the elders" is another aspect of honoring the church family. Several principles are given that guide the Church in the somber responsibility of honoring the elders.

Have someone read 1 Timothy 5 aloud to the group from the ESV.

Discussion Questions

1. What stood out to you from your answers to questions #7-11 in the "Understand and Apply" section?

2. Consider Paul's challenge to Timothy and the elders to "keep yourself pure" (5:22). Most scholars connect the rest of the chapter to this charge (5:23-25).

How could his advice to "use a little wine" (5:23) be connected to this charge for purity? How might this assure Timothy that this use would not tarnish his pursuit of purity?

What are the consequences of leaders whose sin/impurity is evident to others?

What are the consequences of leaders whose sin/impurity is more hidden from others?

How is this the same for good works?

Read 1 Corinthians 4:4-5. How do Paul's words about himself shed light on his explanation about elders' responsibility in living a pure lifestyle?

3. What questions do you still have about 1 Timothy 4? How will you seek answers?

4. Take a few minutes of solitude for everyone to answer these questions individually before sharing them as a group.

What is God saying to you through your study of 1 Timothy 5?

How will you step out in obedience through the power of the Holy Spirit?

Prayer

"Our Father in Heaven, who has adopted us into your family according to the riches of your love and grace, we exalt you and honor you. Thank you for all our brothers and sisters who walk with us in the journey of faith. We know many experience great difficulty in our world, and we pray specifically for the widows who may feel vulnerable and lonely. Reveal to us your plan for our involvement in caring for their needs. Protect and provide for our church leaders. Give them courageous vision, faithful purity, and wise discretion as they lead and serve our churches. May our faith-family display your loving kindness to all those around us.

1 Timothy 6
Finishing Well

"Godliness with contentment is great gain, for we brought nothing into the world, and we cannot take anything out of the world." -1 Timothy 6:1

"Pursue righteousness, godliness, faith, love, steadfastness, gentleness. Fight the good fight of the faith." -1 Timothy 6:11-12a

The Jones. Who are they, and why are we all trying to keep up with them? In today's day and age, it's become increasingly easier for us to compare ourselves to others. As soon as someone gets a new car or purchases a snazzy new pair of shoes, it's posted to their social media for all to see. And as much as we want to be happy for our friends, we often feel something else – jealousy. We feel discontent with our life—our old car, our dull shoes. Even as Christians, it's easy to be caught up in the consumeristic world of MORE.

When God created the world, He called everything He made "good." And Paul says in 1 Timothy 6:17 that God "richly provides us with everything to enjoy." So how should we, as followers of Jesus Christ, think about our material possessions? Should we pursue and enjoy great wealth? Or should we give everything away to the poor so we aren't tempted to be greedy? Today, many people would suggest that one end of this financial spectrum is correct and more holy than the other. This is the type of false teaching that Paul addresses in 1 Timothy 6.

As Paul concludes his first letter to his disciple, Timothy, he continues to address ways that some false teachers were attempting to lead God's people astray. Some had attached financial gain to godly living, so Paul exhorts Timothy to have a healthy view of worldly possessions and to stand against the idol that financial gain can become. Paul closes his letter by calling Timothy to turn from the temptations that lie in front of him and run to Christ as the source of true and lasting wealth.

Read 1 Timothy 6
⇨ Observe

1. Before Paul gets to the primary emphasis of chapter 6, he begins by addressing the issue of slavery (6:1-2). What does he emphasize for the master and the servant? Explain.

2. In 6:3-10 and 6:17-20, Paul addresses the love of money. He begins this section by contrasting sound words (teaching) with questionable motives. What is the outcome of this type of false teaching?

3. Paul writes of godliness with contentment in 6:6-10. In what ways does contentment influence the hearts and minds of believers? In what ways can a lack of contentment cause us to struggle?

4. In 6:11-16, Paul tells Timothy how to stand firm against the temptation of greed. Highlight the many ways believers battle against envy and greed.

5. Paul encourages Timothy to teach the rich not to put their hope in wealth. What are the rich to do instead? Why? (6:18-19)

✋ Understand and Apply

7. In the first two verses of chapter 6, Paul begins by addressing the issue of slavery (6:1-2). The Apostle highlights the fact that every human being is worthy of respect. How might this influence how you view those in positions of authority or those under your guidance/leadership? Explain.

8. In the pastoral letters, when Paul wrote to his disciples, Timothy and Titus, he often wrote of the importance of teaching—and teaching with solid doctrine and proper motives. Read 2 Timothy 2:23-26, 4:2-5, and Titus 1:11. Why is this so important?

9. In 6:6-10, Paul helps believers understand that the opposite of greed is contentment in God. According to the apostle, wealth should not determine the contentment of a follower of Christ. How would you describe your current level of contentment? Draw a line with greed on one end and contentment on the other. Place a dot on the line that describes your current heart posture.

10. Revisit the list of ways Paul highlights for believers to stand firm against the temptation of greed that you detailed in question four. Write down two or three things that you find most helpful. Why?

11. Paul instructs Timothy to encourage wealthy people against haughtiness and arrogance and toward goodness and generosity. How have you been able to use your financial resources for good? Explain. Describe what that experience has taught you about generosity.

✝ Theology Spotlight
IS MONEY GOOD OR EVIL?

In chapter six, Paul returns to the topic of false teachers, this time pointing out those who were trying to be godly only to gain material wealth. Because the desire for money can corrupt anyone, he broadens the lesson to provide all believers with an important understanding of material wealth. A Christian approach to life means acquiring material things can never become the main pursuit.

We must read Paul's proverb carefully: "For the love of money is a root of all kinds of evil" (6:10). First, the problem is the "love of money," and not money itself. Paul's warning to those who "desire to be rich" (6:9) is clearly based upon Jesus' warning of covetousness, clarifying that "one's life does not consist in the abundance of his possessions" (Luke 12:15). Second, it is not the only root of evil, but can be a root. The Apostle John revealed there are three basic desires that bring destruction, "the desires of the flesh and the desires of the eyes and pride in possessions" (1 John 2:16). Third, the love of money is a root of "all kinds of evil." This desire for wealth often entices people to destructive sin and desires that bring spiritual, relational, and physical harm to themselves and others.

Later in this chapter, Paul addressed wealthy believers (6:17-19) with foundational concepts that help us view material possessions properly. God provides wealth, so clearly, it is not sinful to have it. God's purpose in providing wealth is not to promote pride and self-sufficiency but to instill joy in us as we experience His kindness. Out of that joy, we are equipped to influence eternity by being generous with possessions and kind actions (2 Corinthians 9:14).

Essentially, Paul reveals that true wealth is found in unselfish giving rather than self-indulgent possessing. Money and wealth can be a blessing from God used for godly investments or a destructive pursuit opposed to God's ambitions.

Prayer

Use this page to process the Lord's work in your heart through written prayer. Respond to the following prompts or write your own prayer of response.

- Copy the text of 1 Timothy 6:6 below.
- Then reflect on it and your faithfulness in living it.
- Ask God to fill you with contentment in Him.
- Write a prayer detailing what contentment would look like in your life.

FOR LIFE GROUP DISCUSSION

Use the following questions to guide your discussion of chapter 6 in your Life Group meeting.

Icebreaker
Share an example of when you were carefree with your money. Did you buy something significant? Did you give it away for a cause? Explain.

Chapter Review

The final chapter of Paul's letter to Timothy serves to encourage the heart toward the things of God rather than getting caught in the snares of this world, like false teaching and the love of money. Timothy, and all people of faith, are challenged to turn from the temptation of finding contentment in monetary and material wealth. Instead, the person of faith is to fight the good fight by fleeing from pursuing these things and finding contentment in God.

Have someone read 1 Timothy 6 aloud to the group from the ESV.

Discussion Questions

1. What stood out to you from your answers to questions #6-10 in the "Understand & Apply" section?

2. Paul concludes his letter to Timothy with encouragement to "Fight the good fight of faith" and to "Take hold of the eternal life to which you were called" (6:12). **Revisit 6:14-16.** How does Paul's focus on the second coming of Jesus and God's immortal, eternal nature help give Timothy and all readers perspective on the false teachers preaching for financial gain?

Read Matthew 6:19-21 and Luke 14:12-14. How do these passages give you a deeper understanding of why Paul instructs those who are rich to use their money to do good and be generous (6:18)? How does it change your perspective of riches?

3. What questions do you still have about 1 Timothy 6? How will you seek answers?

4. Take a few minutes of solitude for everyone to answer these questions individually before sharing them as a group.

What is God saying to you through your study of 1 Timothy 6?

How will you step out in obedience through the power of the Holy Spirit?

Prayer

Gracious God, you have called us to yourself by faith in your Son, Jesus. And in Him, we have all we need for a life of godliness and contentment. Through the power of the Holy Spirit, may you give us contentment with little or with much.

Grant us the courage to pursue righteousness. Please give us the strength to walk in godliness. Bless us with a deep faith. Empower us to live in your love and offer it freely to others. Help us to remain steadfast. Give us humble and gentle hearts. May our lives be marked by generosity as we seek to walk in your ways. Amen.

For Further Reading

General Resources

ESV Study Bible, Crossway

On the Book of 1 Timothy

"1 Timothy Book Overview" video by The Bible Project at
🖥 **bibleproject.com/explore/video/1-timothy/**

1 & 2 Timothy for You by Phillip Jensen

Christ-Centered Exposition: Exalting Jesus in 1 & 2 Timothy and Titus (Volume 1)
by David Platt, Dr. Daniel L. Akin, and Tony Merida

The Message of 1 Timothy & Titus by John R.W. Stott

On Elders

Gospel Eldership by Robert H. Thune

Church Elders: How to Shepherd God's People like Jesus by Jeramie Rinne

On Deacons

Deacons: How They Serve and Strengthen the Church by Matt Smethurst

Does the Bible Support Female Deacons? Yes by Thomas Schreiner
🖥 **thegospelcoalition.org/article/bible-support-female-deacons-yes/**

Does the Bible Support Female Deacons? No by Guy Waters
🖥 **thegospelcoalition.org/article/bible-support-female-deacons-no/**

On Money

The Treasure Principle by Randy Alcorn

Made in the USA
Monee, IL
15 January 2023

25343423R00036